The Life and Work of
Auguste
Rodin

Richard Tames

www.heinemann.co.uk/library
Visit our website to find out more information about **Heinemann Library** books.

To order:
 Phone 44 (0) 1865 888066
Send a fax to 44 (0) 1865 314091
Visit the Heinemann Bookshop at www.heinemann.co.uk/library to browse our catalogue and order online.

First published in Great Britain by Heinemann Library, Halley Court, Jordan Hill, Oxford OX2 8EJ, part of Harcourt Education.
Heinemann is a registered trademark of Harcourt Education Ltd.

Editorial: Clare Lewis
Design: Jo Hinton-Malivoire and Q2A Creative
Production: Helen McCreath

Printed and bound in China by South China Printing Company

10 digit ISBN 0 431 09888 3
13 digit ISBN 978 0 431 09888 3

10 09 08 07 06
10 9 8 7 6 5 4 3 2 1

British Library Cataloguing in Publication Data
Tames, Richard
The Life and Work of: Auguste Rodin - 2nd edition
730.9'2
A full catalogue record for this book is available from the British Library.

Acknowledgements
The publishers would like to thank the following for permission to reproduce photographs:
Bridgeman Art Library: Musee d'Orsay, Paris p21; Musée Rodin, Paris: pp4, 6, 14, 20, Hélène Moulonguet p7, Adam Rzepka pp5, 9, 13, 18, 25, Charles Aubry pp10,12, Erik and Petra Hesmerg p11, Bruno Jarret p15, Jessie Lipscomb p16, Jêrome Manoukian pp17, 23, Pierre Bonnard p22, Edward Steichen 24, Choumoff p28, Jean de Calan p29; Photo RMN: R G Ojeda p19; Roger-Viollet: Harlingue-Viollet p26; Trip: Christopher Rennie p27

Cover photograph: *Jules Dalou* by Auguste Rodin, reproduced with permission of AKG Images.

The publishers would like to thank Nancy Harris for her assistance in the preparation of this book.

Every effort has been made to contact copyright holders of any material reproduced in this book. Any omissions will be rectified in subsequent printings if notice is given to the publishers.

The paper used to print this book comes from sustainable resources.

Some words in the book are bold, **like this**. You can find out what they mean by looking in the Glossary.

Contents

Who was Auguste Rodin?

Auguste Rodin was a French artist and **sculptor**. He is most famous for the **statues** of people he made out of clay, **bronze**, and **marble**.

Auguste tried to show feelings in his **sculptures**. The people in this sculpture are unhappy because their city in France has been taken over by an English king.

Early years

Auguste was born in Paris, France, on
12 November 1840. This is a photograph of
Auguste at the age of nine with his mother.
He started drawing when he was 10 years old.

Auguste went to a special drawing school
when he was 14. Here are some of his
drawings. He began to make clay models
at the age of 15. His **sculptures** were
based on his drawings of people.

Hard times

Auguste began to earn money making stone decorations for buildings. When his sister died in 1862, he was very sad and he tried to become a **monk**. But he soon returned to his work.

Auguste made art for other people during the day. In the evenings he worked on his own models. He was only 19 when he made this **sculpture** of his father.

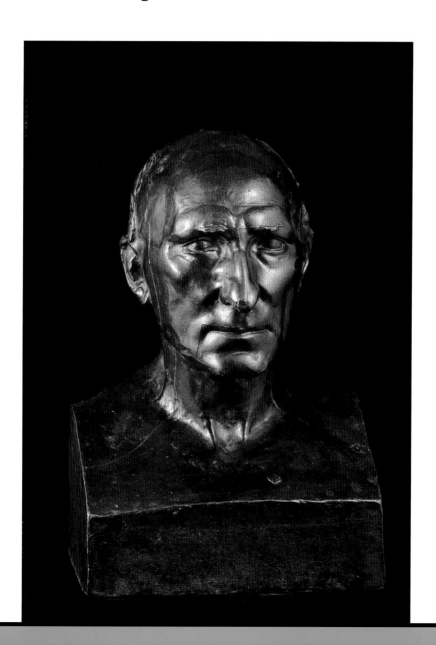

Great changes

In 1864, when he was 24, Auguste met Rose Beuret. She **posed** for him and was his helper for the rest of his life. Auguste got his first **studio**. It was a cold, damp stable.

Auguste and Rose had a son, called
Auguste, in 1866. Auguste made this **bust** of
a young woman the year after he met Rose.
It is called *Young Woman in a Flowered Hat.*

Leaving Paris

Auguste needed to earn money to feed his family. He went to work in Belgium. In 1875 he went to Italy for a year. He **studied** the work of the **sculptor** Michelangelo.

Auguste wanted to become famous. But his *Man with the Broken Nose* was turned down for an important **exhibition**. Many people did not like Auguste's realistic style.

Fame at last

Auguste started to become famous when he was almost 40 years old. His work could bring him trouble too. He made a life-size statue of a soldier, It was called *Age of Bronze*.

Age of Bronze looked so real that some
people said Auguste cheated. After this, he
made his statues bigger or smaller than real
life. He did this to prove he did not cheat.

The work of a lifetime

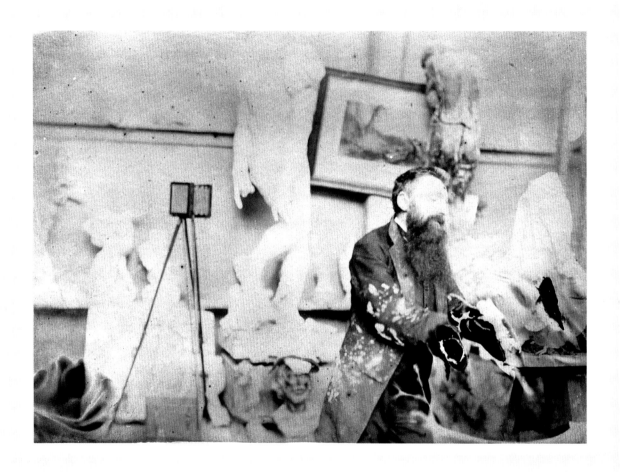

In 1880, Auguste was asked to make a huge doorway for a museum in Paris. He based his drawings for it on the way the Italian poet Dante described Hell. It was called *The Gates of Hell*.

Auguste's most famous **statue**, *The Thinker*, is meant to be Dante. It was meant to go on the top of *The Gates of Hell*.

Camille

This **bust** of Auguste was made by the **sculptor** Camille Claudel in 1888. Auguste liked the bust very much. Camille helped Auguste with his work. She also **posed** for him.

Camille posed for this **sculpture**. It is called *Thought*. Auguste made it in 1888. In it Camille is wearing a hat usually worn by brides in northern France.

A big studio

Auguste moved to Meudon, near Paris. Here he had a big new **studio** with lots of space. He often had up to 50 helpers there. They made **carvings** from his clay models.

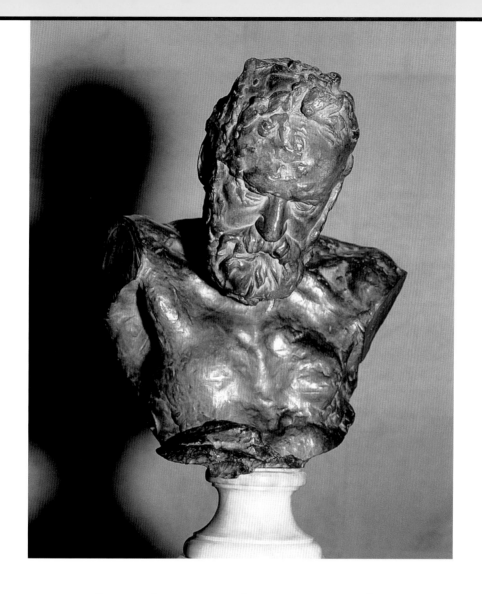

Auguste loved to read. He got a lot
of ideas from books. In 1897 he made
this **bust** of the great French writer
Victor Hugo.

Famous faces

Auguste liked making **busts** of his friends or people he wanted to thank. This picture shows him making a bust of the French **sculptor** Jean Alexandre Falguière.

Auguste showed this **statue** of the French writer Honoré de Balzac in 1898. Auguste read Balzac's books so he could understand him better.

Success

In 1900 Auguste had his first big **exhibition** in Paris. It included over 150 of his **sculptures**. People came from all over the world to see his work.

Auguste called this sculpture *The Cathedral*. He thought that the two hands raised together looked like the pointed arches in cathedrals.

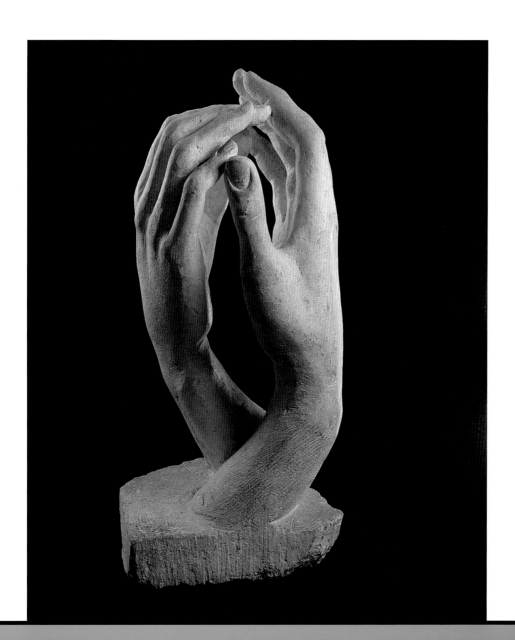

Home and museum

In 1903 Auguste had a **biography** written about him. It was written by the German poet Rainer Maria Rilke. This picture shows Rainer with Rose and Auguste and their dogs outside their house.

Rainer invited Auguste to the Hotel Biron in Paris. This building became Auguste's home. Today it is a museum. Many people come here to see Auguste's work.

Last days

Rose died on 14 February 1917. Auguste died on 17 November 1917. They were buried together at Meudon under a copy of Auguste's **statue** of *The Thinker*.

When Auguste died, *The Gates of Hell* was still unfinished. It can be seen at the Rodin Museum in Paris.

Timeline

1840   Rene-Francois-Auguste Rodin is born on 12 November.

1854   Auguste goes to drawing school.

1857   Auguste fails to get into art college.

1862–63   Auguste tries to become a **monk**.

1864   Auguste meets Rose Beuret.

1870   Auguste joins the army.

1871   Auguste leaves the army and moves to Belgium.

1875–76   Auguste travels in Italy to **study** art.

1877   Auguste moves back to Paris.

1880   Auguste is asked to make *The Gates of Hell.*

1897   Auguste moves to Meudon.

1900   Auguste shows 150 **sculptures** at a Paris **exhibition**.

1903   Rainer Maria Rilke writes Auguste's **biography**.

1908   King Edward VII of England visits Auguste's **studio**.

1914   Auguste publishes a book on the **cathedrals** of France.

1914–18   First World War.

1917   Auguste dies on 17 November.

Glossary

biography story of a person's life

bronze metal made of tin and copper

bust statue of a head and shoulders

carvings object carved (cut out) of wood or rock

cathedral main church of a big city

exhibition show of art in public

marble special kind of limestone rock

monk man who devotes his whole life to his religion

pose stand or sit in a certain way while someone paints or draws you

sculptor person who makes statues or carvings

sculpture statue or carving

statue carved, moulded, or sculpted figure of a person or animal

studio special room or building where an artist works

study to learn about a subject

More books to read

The Children's Book of Art, Rosie Dickens (Usborne Publishing, 2005)

More sculptures to see

Copies of Auguste Rodin's work can also be seen in:

 Victoria and Albert Museum, London

The Burrell Collection, Glasgow

National Museum of Wales, Cardiff

Aberdeen Art Gallery.

Index